OLYMPICS

Richard Platt

Illustrated by Manuela Cappon

KINGFISHER
NEW YORK

World timeline

The world's greatest, fastest, brightest sports show comes around only once every four years. Great cities take turns to host this two-week-long event. The Olympic Games combine the razzmatazz of a carnival with the serious business of world-class competition. They are so gripping that even people with no interest in sports turn on the TV.

The longest running race of the Games, the marathon, is named in honor of a famous Greek battle.

- ● Red dots mark the locations of Games that you can read about in this book.
- ○ Red circles mark the host cities of other Summer Games.

Arctic Ocean

North America

Lillehammer, 1994

Helsinki, 1952

Stockholm, 1912

Mosco... 1980

Europe

London, 1908, 1948, and 2012

Amsterdam, 1928

Berlin, 1936

Paris, 1900 and 1924

Antwerp, 1920

Munich, 1972

Montreal, 1976

Los Angeles, 1932 and 1984

St. Louis, 1904

Rome, 1960

Barcelona, 1992

Athens, 1896 and 2004

Atlanta, 1996

Atlantic Ocean

Pacific Ocean

Africa

Mexico City, 1968

This spectacular event—contested by amateur, unpaid athletes—started just over 100 years ago, yet it follows a 2,800-year-old tradition. The *original* Olympics began in ancient Greece, when that country was just a group of warring cities. While their athletes raced, Greek soldiers put down their swords. The revival of the Olympics in 1896 aimed to restore the same peaceful spirit.

South America

Rio de Janeiro, 2016

Before the statue of thunderbolt-throwing god Zeus, ancient Greek athletes swore they would not cheat.

2

Southern Ocean

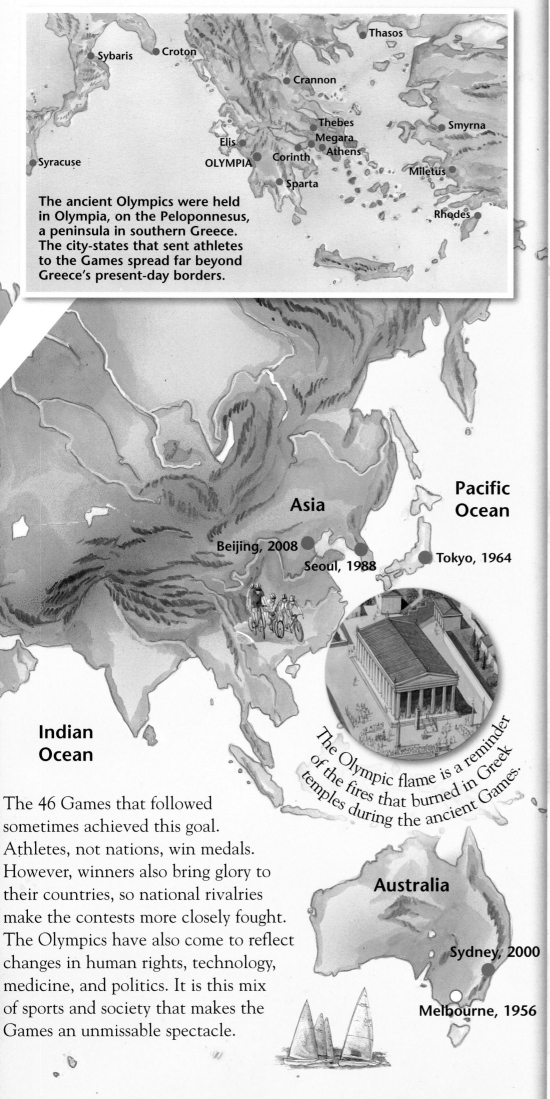

The ancient Olympics were held in Olympia, on the Peloponnesus, a peninsula in southern Greece. The city-states that sent athletes to the Games spread far beyond Greece's present-day borders.

Map labels: Sybaris, Croton, Thasos, Crannon, Syracuse, Elis, OLYMPIA, Corinth, Sparta, Thebes, Megara, Athens, Smyrna, Miletus, Rhodes

Asia

Pacific Ocean

Beijing, 2008

Seoul, 1988

Tokyo, 1964

Indian Ocean

The Olympic flame is a reminder of the fires that burned in Greek temples during the ancient Games.

Australia

Sydney, 2000

Melbourne, 1956

The 46 Games that followed sometimes achieved this goal. Athletes, not nations, win medals. However, winners also bring glory to their countries, so national rivalries make the contests more closely fought. The Olympics have also come to reflect changes in human rights, technology, medicine, and politics. It is this mix of sports and society that makes the Games an unmissable spectacle.

Timeline

776 B.C. First Olympic Games held in Olympia, with a men's 200-m sprint.

490 B.C. Messenger Pheidippides runs 26 mi. (42km) from Sparta to Athens with news of a Greek victory at the Battle of Marathon.

388 B.C. First recorded attempt to bribe an Olympic judge.

12 B.C. King Herod of Judea becomes president of the Olympics.

A.D. 261 Last regular Olympic Games.

A.D. 393 Roman emperor Theodosius I bans the "pagan" Olympic Games.

A.D. 1850 Start of "Olympian Games" in Much Wenlock, Shropshire, U.K.

A.D. 1859 Greek sports enthusiasts try to revive the ancient Olympics, with only Greek athletes taking part.

A.D. 1893 French Baron Pierre de Coubertin sets up the International Olympic Committee (IOC), with other rich noblemen as members.

A.D. 1896 First modern Olympics, for amateurs only, held in Athens, Greece.

A.D. 1900 Second Games takes place as part of the French *Exposition Universelle* in Paris. Women compete for the first time, in tennis and golf.

A.D. 1904 Winners receive gold, silver, and bronze medals for the first time.

A.D. 1914 de Coubertin designs a five-ring symbol to represent the five inhabited continents (he counts North America and South America as one). World War I begins, causing the 1916 Berlin Olympics to be canceled.

A.D. 1924 First Winter Games held, in Chamonix, France.

A.D. 1939 World War II starts, so the 1940 and 1944 Games are canceled.

A.D. 1956 Winter Olympics in Cortina d'Ampezzo, Italy, are the first to be internationally televised.

A.D. 1960 First Games for disabled athletes held after the Rome Olympics.

A.D. 1972 Terrorists kill 11 members of the Israeli team at the Munich Games.

A.D. 1980 61 nations boycott the Moscow Games to protest the host nation's invasion of Afghanistan.

A.D. 1984 Communist nations boycott the Los Angeles Games in revenge for the 1980 boycott.

A.D. 1988 Professional athletes finally admitted to most Olympic sports.

A.D. 1998 IOC members resign after accepting bribes to vote for Salt Lake City's bid to host the Winter Olympics.

A.D. 2004 The Athens marathon retraces Pheidippides' 2,500-year-old run.

A.D. 2008 At $43 billion, the Beijing Olympics are the costliest so far.

What do these dates mean?
B.C. means "before Christ." For example, 100 B.C. refers to 100 years before the birth of Jesus Christ, as traditionally calculated. A.D. means "anno Domini" (medieval Latin for "year of our Lord") and refers to all dates after the birth of Christ.

Timeline axis: 776 B.C. · 500 B.C. · 100 B.C. · A.D. 100 · A.D. 1800 · A.D. 1900 · A.D. 1950 · A.D. 2000

Contents

In the pages of this book, you can read the thrilling story of the modern Olympics. Starting with a small contest in Greece, they soon grew into a major international event. As host cities competed to stage the best Games ever, athletes trained, struggled—and even cheated—to win gold. And when TV gave the Games an audience of millions, they attracted profit, protests, and sometimes tragedy.

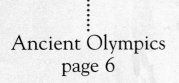

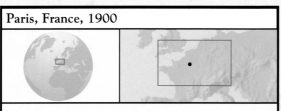

Paris, France, 1900

A locator map shows where the Games took place, with information on events, teams, and medals won.

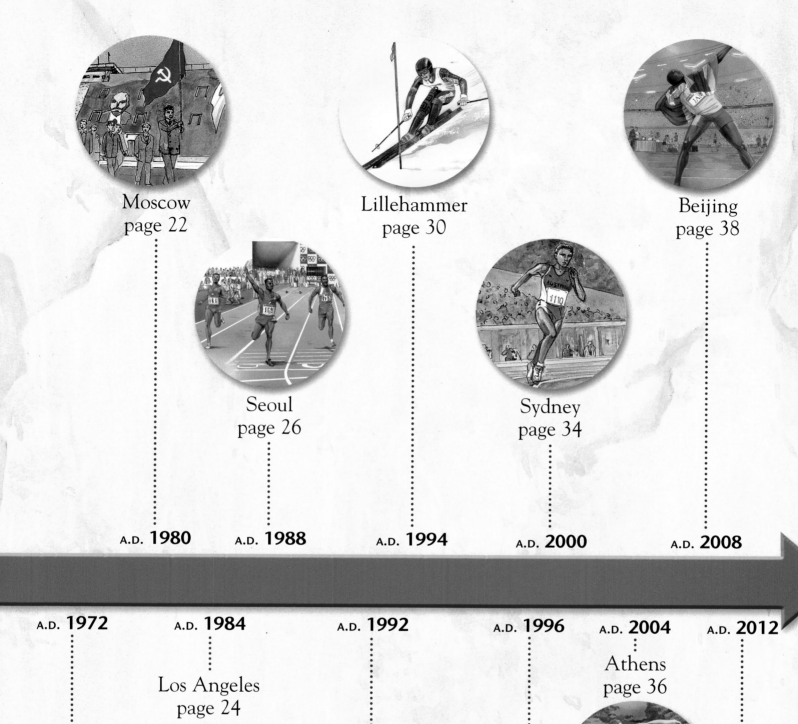

Reviving the Games

Twenty athletes line up for a footrace. Around them, the smell of cheap food fills the summer air. Watching expectantly on a hillside, a huge crowd cheers as the race begins. This is no modern scene. It's an ancient race in Olympia, Greece. The Olympic Games began here as a simple running race in 776 B.C. to honor the Greek god Zeus. It grew into a huge attraction in which rival Greek cities competed in track and field events, fighting, and chariot racing every four years.

the Olympia track is 112 mi. (180km) from the Greek capital, Athens

Victorious athletes win a crown of olive leaves, but no precious gold or silver medals.

the Games attract hordes of seedy peddlers, gamblers, and good-time girls

spectators from warring Greek states vow not to fight during the events

spectators watch from a low hill

only judges and celebrities have seats, in a special enclosure

athletes race without clothes

statues found while restoring the stadium decorate the track in 1896, too

only men can take part—or stand and watch

it was not uncommon for judges to accept bribes from athletes

footraces are the very first Olympic events

The English town of Much Wenlock revives the Olympic Games as early as 1850.

Interest in the Olympics fades, but the contest is not forgotten. There are "revival" games in France, Great Britain, and Greece. Then, in 1894, wealthy French scholar Baron Pierre de Coubertin starts the International Olympic Committee (IOC). He wants to recreate the Olympics to encourage athletes worldwide.

Olympia, ancient Greece, 700s B.C.

Two years later, the first modern Olympic Games begin in Athens. It's just a small event in which 241 athletes compete. It is largely ignored by the world's press. But it achieves Baron de Coubertin's aim of using sports to bring rival nations together. As the competitors leave Athens at the end, they say, "See you in Paris in four years!"

Athens, Greece, 1896

- **Number of events:** 43, across 9 sports
- **Number of competing nations:** 14
- **Most gold medals:** 11 (U.S.A.)
- **Number of athletes competing:** 241

people without tickets watch from surrounding hills

Baron Pierre de Coubertin (1863–1937) promotes school sports before backing the Olympics.

The 1896 Games are held in sight of the Parthenon, the famous temple of the goddess Athena.

Tourist John Boland joins the British team on a whim and wins a gold medal for tennis.

marble seats are restored for the Games

the Panathinaiko Stadium is more than 2,000 years old

women can watch but not take part

some athletes complain that the track is too soft

sharp bends in the short track slow the runners

from the most distant seats, the athletes look like "agitated insects"

Panathinaiko Stadium, Athens, 1896

7

Paris 1900

The revival of the Olympics in Athens encourages founder Pierre de Coubertin. Now he wants the Games to come to his home city, Paris. He persuades French leaders to stage the Olympics as part of a giant exhibition, the *Exposition Universelle*, in 1900. It is a big mistake. The show's organizer hates sports. The program lists Olympic events alongside firefighting contests and pigeon races. The ice skaters are billed as part of a show of knives and forks.

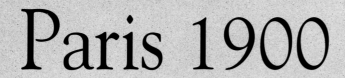

American Alvin Kraenzlein wins four individual events: an Olympic record that still stands today.

runners glimpse the famous Arc de Triomphe in the distance as they cross the Avenue de la Grande Armée

the Paris Métro opens for the first time on the day of the race

streetcar system

Close to the Paris slaughterhouse, marathon runners pick their way through sheep and cattle.

most spectators do not even know a race is planned today

Avenue de la Grande Armée

normal street traffic gets in the runners' way

the runners make a clockwise circuit of the old city of Paris

Auguste Marchais

Georges Touquet-Daunis

Frenchmen Marchais and Touquet-Daunis—the two leaders at this point—never actually complete the race

Everything about the Games is a mess. There is no opening ceremony—or even a stadium. Athletes compete on bumpy lawns in the Bois de Boulogne, a Paris park where javelins get stuck in trees. Swimming events are held in the fast-flowing, polluted Seine River.

In the marathon, just 16 runners tear around the ancient walls of Paris in sweltering summer heat. None of the roads is closed for the race. Competitors get lost and dodge passersby. When a Frenchman—Michél Theato—wins, the American team accuses him of cheating. It is chaos, but the Paris Games are a success in one important way: they keep the Olympic dream alive.

Built to celebrate an earlier Exposition Universelle, the Eiffel Tower is only 11 years old.

Paris, France, 1900

- **Number of events:** 95, across 20 sports
- **Number of competing nations:** 24
- **Most gold medals:** 27 (France)
- **Number of athletes competing:** 997

Avenue de Malakoff

the watching crowds include hardly any race officials

some of the runners wear hats to keep off the fierce sun

sweat pours off the runners in the searing summer heat

sneakers have not been invented yet, so runners wear slippery, leather-soled shoes

the heat has already forced four runners out of the race

cyclists pedal alongside the competitors

Berlin 1936

In a giant, brand-new stadium in Berlin, Germany's leader Adolf Hitler beams down at an enormous Olympic crowd. As a National Socialist (or "Nazi"), he believes that white European people are better than all others. Now his country is hosting the Olympic Games, and he is confident that German athletes will prove him right. Hitler has come to watch the final of the men's 100-m race. His eyes are on Erich Borchmeyer—the only German running.

Hitler hates to see Germans racing "blacks and Jews" but wants the glamour of the Games.

radio reporters in the press box broadcast commentary in 28 languages

Hitler watches from a celebrity stand high up above the finish line

The starting gun echoes around the stadium. The sprinters lunge forward, their limbs a blur of speed. One man is clearly a winner from the very start. African-American Jesse Owens has a striding pace that leaves Borchmeyer far behind. It takes the black athlete only 10.3 seconds to win a gold medal. Furious, Hitler stalks from the stadium.

German fans cheer Erich Borchmeyer, but he does not win a medal

American Ralph Metcalf is only one-tenth of a second behind Owens

Dutch runner Martinus Osendarp comes in third, finishing in 10.5 seconds

the track is sunk 40 ft. (12m) below ground level to make more space for spectators

American Jesse Owens leads the 100-m sprint easily

Basketball is new to the 1936 Olympics: playing in torrential rain, the U.S.A. wins gold in the final.

Owens's success shows that athletes can compete in the Olympic Games as equals, whatever their skin color. Americans are triumphant about the victory and claim that Hitler "snubbed" Owens. But the gold medal does not end racial prejudice. For when this Olympic champion returns home, his black skin will still prevent him from competing in many races.

During the Games, Nazi "swastika" flags are flown in streets all over Germany.

the gigantic stadium holds 110,000 people

Berlin, Germany, 1936

- **Number of events:** 129, across 24 sports
- **Number of competing nations:** 49
- **Most gold medals:** 38 (Germany)
- **Number of athletes competing:** 3,963

TV cameras beam the Games live to 28 giant screens around the city

Lennart Strandberg

Frank Wykoff

Gymnast Alfred Schwarzmann is a German Olympic hero, winning three gold and two bronze medals.

Owens's rivals strain to catch him

London 1948

After the Berlin Olympics, a long and brutal war tears the world apart. Survival, not sports, is on everyone's mind. Two Olympic Games are canceled. London is chosen as the host for the 1948 Olympics, but its residents—like many other Britons—are tired and poor. It is clear that their country cannot afford the grandeur that the world admired in Germany 12 years earlier. It will have to be a "make-do-and-mend" Olympics.

Short on everything, the British hosts look for ways to create a spectacular show from nothing. Schools and army barracks become temporary homes for the competitors. There is no money to build new stadiums, so workers repair an old one in Wembley, in northwest London. Even this proves hard—scaffolding, paint, and cement run out, and cinders from household stoves provide the track with a "new" running surface.

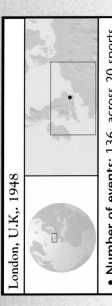

London, U.K., 1948

- **Number of events:** 136, across 20 sports
- **Number of competing nations:** 59
- **Most gold medals:** 38 (U.S.A.)
- **Number of athletes competing:** 4,104

The stadium will be demolished in 2003, along with its famous twin towers, to make way for a new one.

the crowd bakes in 93°F (34°C) sunshine—the hottest day for 37 years

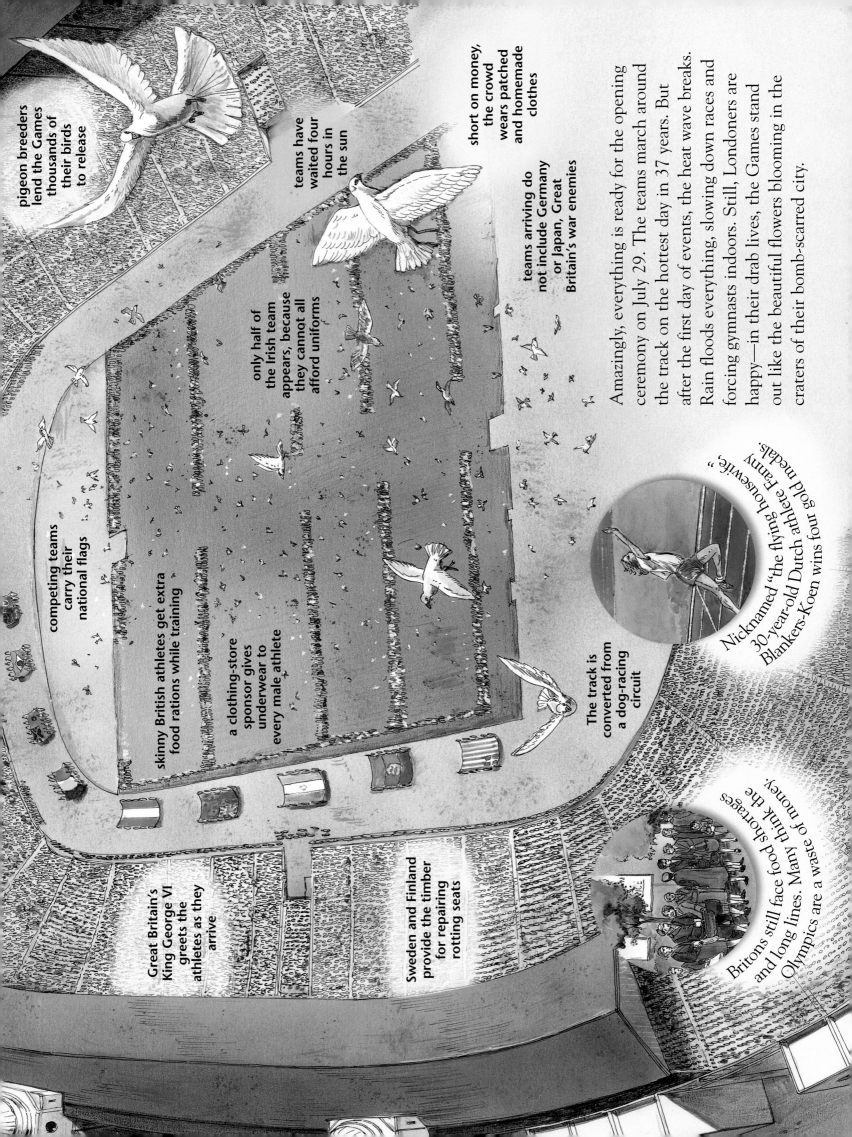

pigeon breeders lend the Games thousands of their birds to release

teams have waited four hours in the sun

short on money, the crowd wears patched and homemade clothes

teams arriving do not include Germany or Japan, Great Britain's war enemies

competing teams carry their national flags

only half of the Irish team appears, because they cannot all afford uniforms

skinny British athletes get extra food rations while training

a clothing-store sponsor gives underwear to every male athlete

The track is converted from a dog-racing circuit

Great Britain's King George VI greets the athletes as they arrive

Sweden and Finland provide the timber for repairing rotting seats

Amazingly, everything is ready for the opening ceremony on July 29. The teams march around the track on the hottest day in 37 years. But after the first day of events, the heat wave breaks. Rain floods everything, slowing down races and forcing gymnasts indoors. Still, Londoners are happy—in their drab lives, the Games stand out like the beautiful flowers blooming in the craters of their bomb-scarred city.

Nicknamed "the flying housewife," 30-year-old Dutch athlete Fanny Blankers-Koen wins four gold medals.

Britons still face food shortages and long lines. Many think the Olympics are a waste of money.

Rome 1960

Two thousand years ago, the Roman Games meant a desperate battle to the death between slave gladiators. When Rome hosts the Olympics in 1960, the competition is just as fierce, though athletes now fight for medals, not for their lives! The city spends lavishly to make the Games a success. A vast athletes' village replaces a slum. Six gleaming new stadiums rise around Rome.

Rome, Italy, 1960

- **Number of events:** 150, across 19 sports
- **Number of competing nations:** 83
- **Most gold medals:** 43 (U.S.S.R.)
- **Number of athletes competing:** 5,338

the basilica stands on the forum (city square) of ancient Rome

bouts are scheduled for morning and evening to avoid the sun's scorching heat

special lighting in the arches illuminates the bouts

Russia's female gymnasts scoop most of the medals—a victory for one of the Cold War superpowers.

Greco-Roman wrestling has been part of the Olympics since the first modern Games

Romans are proud of their history, and they use ruined monuments as spectacular settings for the modern Games. Ethiopian barefoot runner Abede Bikila wins the marathon under an ancient emperor's arch. Russian gymnasts scoop gold medals in a restored bathhouse. And under the soaring arches of the Basilica of Maxentius, where Roman councilors once met, wrestlers compete for gold.

wrestlers from 46 nations fight where a huge statue of Roman Emperor Constantine once stood

the basilica is more than 1,650 years old

dressing rooms are behind the platforms

when the basilica was completed in the early A.D. 300s, it was the largest structure in the world

Turkey is the champion, winning seven wrestling golds

Danish cyclist Knud Jensen falls during the road race and later dies. Drugs are found in his system.

The Paralympics are held for the first time, with events including archery and wheelchair basketball.

wrestlers fight on mattressed (springy) platforms

a Bulgarian wrestler is kicked out of the competition for a deliberate fall

bouts include both freestyle and Greco-Roman wrestling

Despite the harmony of the Games, some of the athletes' rivalries continue outside the stadium. The United States and the Soviet Union are competing for power in the Cold War. Whichever nation's team wins the most medals will claim a political victory. The German athletes, however, show the power of the Olympic ideal. They compete as a single team, even though a border has split their nation into East and West since 1945.

Tokyo 1964

High up above a gigantic sports stadium, a young athlete lifts a flaming torch. A plume of fire bursts from the Olympic cauldron, and below him the vast crowd erupts in cheers and applause. Even before a single race is run, it's a triumph for Japan. For this is the first Asian Olympics.

Tokyo, Japan, 1964

- **Number of events:** 163, across 21 sports
- **Number of competing nations:** 93
- **Most gold medals:** 36 (U.S.A.)
- **Number of athletes competing:** 5,151

5,700 competitors and officials watch from ground level

the Japanese emperor stands in the royal box

the opening ceremonies take place on a small stage below the royal box

For the first time, judo is included in the program. Japan wins gold in three of the four categories.

trumpeters sound a fanfare after the emperor declares the Games open

These Games mark Japan's recovery from the terrible destruction of World War II. The wiry figure lighting the flame is Yoshinori Sakai. He was born in Hiroshima on the day the United States dropped an atomic bomb on the city. The bomb's monstrous explosion helped end the war, but it destroyed Hiroshima. Sakai's lighting of the flame remembers the past, but in all other ways, the Tokyo Olympics look forward to a bright new future for Japan.

75,000 spectators fill the stands

The Games are the best prepared and best connected so far. Computers keep track of races and records, such as U.K. sprinter Ann Packer's world record in the 800m. The world's fastest train brings visitors to watch champions such as American Don Schollander, who wins four golds in the swimming pool. Even a satellite relays live TV coverage of the Games.

Satellites beam the drama of the Tokyo Olympics to television audiences all over the world.

military aircraft trace the Olympic rings in the sky

flags of 94 competing nations fly above the stadium

an electronic scoreboard displays translations of the speeches

sprayers above the spectators squirt perfume of chrysanthemum (a flower)

schoolgirls, each ving 40 balloons, t their tethers to release them

propane gas fuels the flame in the cauldron

the torch flame burns for only 14 minutes

a runners' relay has carried the flame through 14 countries, across 14,000 mi. (23,000km)

Soviet gymnast Larissa Latynina ins two golds, bringing her total mpic medal count to 18—a record.

17

Mexico City 1968

American Tommie Smith seems like a perfect Olympic champion when he races in the 200m. He wins in less than 20 seconds—a feat no athlete has achieved before. But despite his victory, he is angry. He tells a journalist, "On the track, you are the fastest man in the world. But in the dressing room, you are nothing more than a dirty negro."

This is the first time that the Games have been held in a developing nation.

press photographs will make the protest famous the following day

Mexican spectators are delighted by the embarrassment the runners cause

High jumper Dick Fosbury (U.S.A.) uses a new technique that becomes known as the Fosbury Flop.

Mexico City, Mexico, 1968

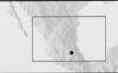

- **Number of events:** 172, across 20 sports
- **Number of competing nations:** 112
- **Most gold medals:** 45 (U.S.A.)
- **Number of athletes competing:** 5,516

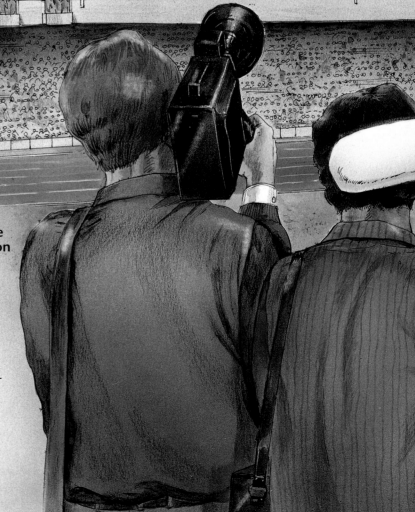

white American spectators boo at the men's salute

TV cameras beam the sensation to 400 million viewers worldwide

So when Smith and his teammate John Carlos step onto the podium to receive gold and bronze medals, they make a silent protest. As the U.S. anthem plays, both raise a gloved fist in a "black power" salute. Their protest about racism—in sports and society—shocks all who see it. Furious officials order the runners home. Neither will run a major race again.

the runners have turned to face the American flag

all three athletes will receive death threats for their protest

Smith is saying a silent prayer as he looks down

Australian Peter Norman wears an OPHR patch to show that he agrees with the other two runners

Carlos makes a left-handed salute because they are sharing a pair of gloves

Carlos wears a string of beads to represent black Americans who have been lynched (illegally executed)

To many black people, however, the two men are heroes. Their gesture is part of the huge American civil rights movement. Three months earlier, racists murdered the movement's leader, Martin Luther King, Jr. Now, on the podium in Mexico, Smith and Carlos make the civil rights message into world news. They also show that keeping politics out of the Olympics is an impossible fantasy.

During the construction of the Olympic Village, an Aztec pyramid is unearthed.

the athletes have taken off their shoes to represent the poverty of many African Americans

official David Burghley, who awards the medals, won Olympic gold in the 400-m hurdles 40 years earlier

19

Munich 1972

The Olympic Village in Munich is peaceful in the early morning of September 5. Thousands of athletes are dreaming of glory. But for the Israeli team, the dream is about to become a nightmare. At 4:30 A.M., Arab terrorists burst into the Israeli apartments and take nine hostages. Two Israelis who fight off the attack die in a hail of gunfire.

a TV camera on this broadcast tower focuses on the besieged apartment

Munich, West Germany, 1972

- **Number of events:** 195, across 23 sports
- **Number of competing nations:** 121
- **Most gold medals:** 50 (U.S.S.R.)
- **Number of athletes competing:** 7,134

organizers hope the low-key security will erase memories of the 1936 Olympics

plans to shoot the terrorists in a Village parking lot fail

the Israeli apartment is in Connollystrasse, near the edge of the Village

helicopters take off from open ground in the Village

buses carry the terrorists and hostages to the helicopters

terrorists scaled an unguarded fence near their target

American swimmer Mark Spitz collects seven gold medals at the Munich Games.

The terrorists are from Black September, a Palestinian guerrilla group from the refugee camps on Israel's borders. They fled their homes in 1948, when armed Jewish settlers drove them from Palestine, renaming it Israel. Now they want revenge. They threaten to kill their nine hostages unless Israel releases 200 Arab prisoners.

many athletes elsewhere in the Village ignored the crisis in Connollystrasse

Marathon winner Frank Shorter (U.S.A.) says that to cancel the Games would be to give in to terrorism.

20

the Games start again after only a day of mourning for the victims

The light, acrylic-glass roof of the Olympic Stadium was designed to look like the Alps mountains.

the main stadium

hoods hide the terrorists' identities

the terrorists are armed with pistols, grenades, and AK-47 assault rifles

the terrified hostages are blindfolded

BUNDESGRENZSCHUTZ

The world watches in shock as images of the wrecked helicopters are shown on television.

police seal off the Village after the hostage-taking

the helicopters head toward the military airfield in Fürstenfeldbruck

The Israeli government refuses, so the Germans promise to fly the terrorists and hostages to a friendly Arab nation. The offer is a trick: snipers at the airport prepare to kill the terrorists. But the plan goes horribly wrong. In an hour-long battle, the terrorists kill the hostages. Though the sporting events resume, the Olympics will never be the same.

Moscow 1980

As athletes in Moscow prepare to battle for medals, a deadlier war rages 2,100 mi. (3,400km) away. Soldiers of the Soviet Union (Russia and its allies) are fighting to control Afghanistan. The war splits world opinion. The United States leads the opposition, giving guns and money to a guerrilla army fighting Soviet rule. The U.S. uses the Olympics as a weapon, too, boycotting (staying out of) the Games in the Soviet capital.

special lane dividers and deep water reduce splashing, which cuts speed

Russian Aleksandr Chaev takes the silver medal

Cosmonauts in the *Salyut 6* space station greet the crowd in a video link on the stadium scoreboard.

Australian Max Metzker wins the bronze medal

beneath the swimming pool is a children's play pool and gym

officials and the media have as many seats as the public

More than 60 other nations join the American boycott. Their Olympic teams are disappointed and bitter. Their athletes have trained for years to be in peak condition for the Games. Now they are missing what may be their only chance to win gold. However, for athletes of attending nations, the boycott is an advantage. It removes their toughest opponents from the races.

The boycott is most obvious in the pool. In earlier Olympics, U.S. swimmers had few rivals. With no Americans in the water, other nations take the lead. One swimmer, though, needs no special help. Nobody in the world can swim farther and faster than Russian Vladimir Salnikov. In a record-breaking race, he is the first man ever to swim 1,500m in less than 15 minutes.

the crowd begins cheering when Salnikov breaks the record

Cheers from Salnikov's fans distract Soviet Aleksandr Portnov, spoiling his dive in the pool next door.

the crowd shouts, "*Molodiet*"—Russian for "courageous"— on their hero's victory

the springboard final is taking place in the diving pool in the room next door

British runner Steve Ovett wins the 800m, beating rival Sebastian Coe but then loses to him in the 1,500m.

the 30-length race is the longest in the Olympics

Salnikov finishes half a pool length ahead of his nearest rival

Moscow, Soviet Union (now Russia), 1980

- **Number of events:** 203, across 23 sports
- **Number of competing nations:** 80
- **Most gold medals:** 80 (U.S.S.R.)
- **Number of athletes competing:** 5,179

23

Los Angeles 1984

Inside a packed stadium in the United States' second-largest city, a tiny figure sprints nimbly toward a vaulting horse. She leaps from the springboard and tumbles in the air with a grace and elegance that is almost magical. Spectators roar their approval, and the judges share the crowd's enthusiasm. American gymnast Mary Lou Retton, only 16 years old, scores a perfect 10 points and wins a gold medal.

For watching Americans, Mary Lou's victory is long overdue. Usually, eastern Europeans scoop gymnastic golds, but most of them are not at the Games, staging a boycott that mirrors Moscow four years earlier. Romania, the only eastern European nation to ignore the Soviet ban, comes in third in the medals table. But the U.S. teams are the ones that benefit most, winning a total of 174 medals.

The Romanian team gets warm applause for defying the boycott. Their weightlifters win eight medals.

gymnastics events take place in the indoor Pauley Pavilion

Los Angeles, California, U.S., 1984

- **Number of events:** 221, across 25 sports
- **Number of competing nations:** 140
- **Most gold medals:** 83 (U.S.A.)
- **Number of athletes competing:** 6,829

in the all-around finals, gymnasts perform on the uneven bars, the balance beam, and on the floor

keeping her legs straight and together adds power to Mary Lou's jump

gymnasts perform on a 3-ft. (1-m)-high platform reused from the Montreal Olympics

the run-up to the vault gives Mary Lou the speed she needs for takeoff

a springboard just before the vault helps gymnasts get airborne

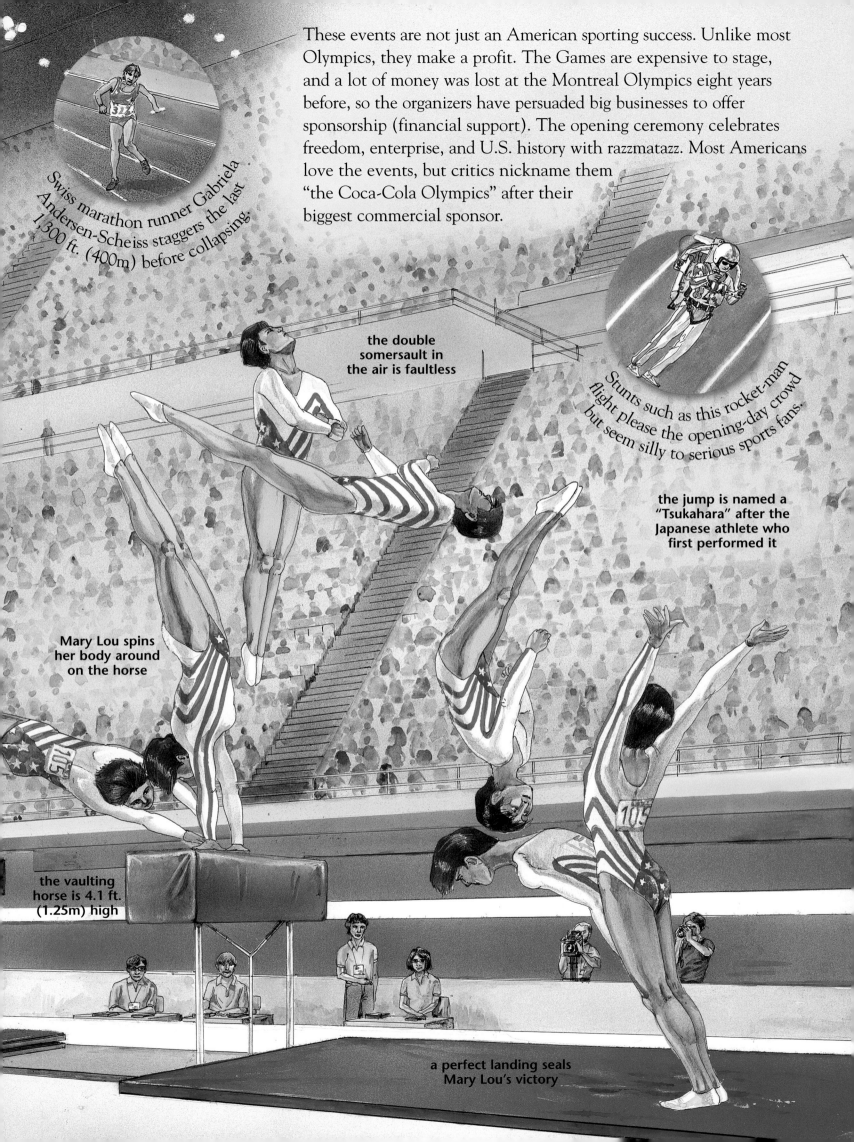

These events are not just an American sporting success. Unlike most Olympics, they make a profit. The Games are expensive to stage, and a lot of money was lost at the Montreal Olympics eight years before, so the organizers have persuaded big businesses to offer sponsorship (financial support). The opening ceremony celebrates freedom, enterprise, and U.S. history with razzmatazz. Most Americans love the events, but critics nickname them "the Coca-Cola Olympics" after their biggest commercial sponsor.

Swiss marathon runner Gabriela Andersen-Scheiss staggers the last 1,300 ft. (400m) before collapsing.

Stunts such as this rocket-man flight please the opening-day crowd but seem silly to serious sports fans.

the double somersault in the air is faultless

the jump is named a "Tsukahara" after the Japanese athlete who first performed it

Mary Lou spins her body around on the horse

the vaulting horse is 4.1 ft. (1.25m) high

a perfect landing seals Mary Lou's victory

Seoul 1988

For the crowd in Seoul's packed stadium, the shortest track-and-field event is the most electrifying. Spectators have waited for months and traveled for days to watch just ten seconds of action. Everyone's eyes are on the eight athletes at the starting line. The winner of this race, the 100-m sprint, will not only get a gold medal—he can also claim to be the "world's fastest man."

In the first Olympic table-tennis competitions, South Korea wins the men's singles and women's doubles.

20 previous races narrowed down 103 runners to only eight in the final

TV crews record every dramatic moment

Ben Johnson raises his arm in victory

Florence Griffith-Joyner (U.S.A.) wins the 100-m and 200-m women's sprints, setting still-unbeaten records.

Desai Williams takes sixth place after fellow Canadian Johnson is disqualified

Johnson pulls ahead of Lewis after 60m

Johnson and Lewis have been rivals for years

For American Carl Lewis and Canadian Ben Johnson, it is a very personal battle. Lewis won gold in 1984. Johnson is eager to take it this time. At the starting gun, the two men surge from the blocks together, as if joined by invisible wires. Within six seconds, though, Johnson takes the lead, winning in an astonishing 9.79 seconds. After the race, he brags triumphantly, "This record will last 50 years."

all four leaders finish in less than ten seconds

It barely lasts two days. Tests reveal that Johnson has taken stanozolol, a muscle-boosting drug banned in sports. Disqualified and stripped of his medal, he flies home to Canada. Carl Lewis takes gold, but for him and the other medalists, it is a sour victory. Sports officials have been battling for years to stop drug use, and Johnson's drug-fueled run is a shaming setback.

Canadian sailor Lawrence Lemieux gives up a silver medal to rescue shipwrecked rivals from the water.

American Calvin Smith gains bronze after Johnson's disqualification

Great Britain's Linford Christie wins silver after officials strip Johnson of his medal

Carl Lewis finishes the race in 9.92 seconds

Lewis is later awarded the gold medal

Seoul, South Korea, 1988

- **Number of events:** 237, across 27 sports
- **Number of competing nations:** 153
- **Most gold medals:** 55 (U.S.S.R.)
- **Number of athletes competing:** 8,391

Barcelona 1992

On the sunlit seafront of Spain's second city, an ocean park has replaced derelict buildings. Apartments and arenas stand where there were once only factories and docks. When the Barcelona Olympics begin, these sparkling new buildings echo with foreign accents, as athletes and spectators from 169 countries fill the Olympic Village and the new stadiums.

Spanish Paralympian archer Antonio Rebollo lights the Olympic cauldron by firing a flaming arrow above it

Soling-class yachts are 27 ft. (8m) long and have a crew of three

In the blue Mediterranean waters, the world's best yachtsmen use their skills and strength to squeeze the last bit of speed from their boats. Among them is Prince Don Felipe of Bourbon, heir to the Spanish throne. He is competing in the Soling-class yacht races as an ordinary athlete, just like the 9,355 others who have come to Barcelona in search of glory.

Spanish prince Don Felipe of Bourbon crews one of the boats

also on the prince's boat are skipper Fernando Leon and helmsman Alfredo Vazquez

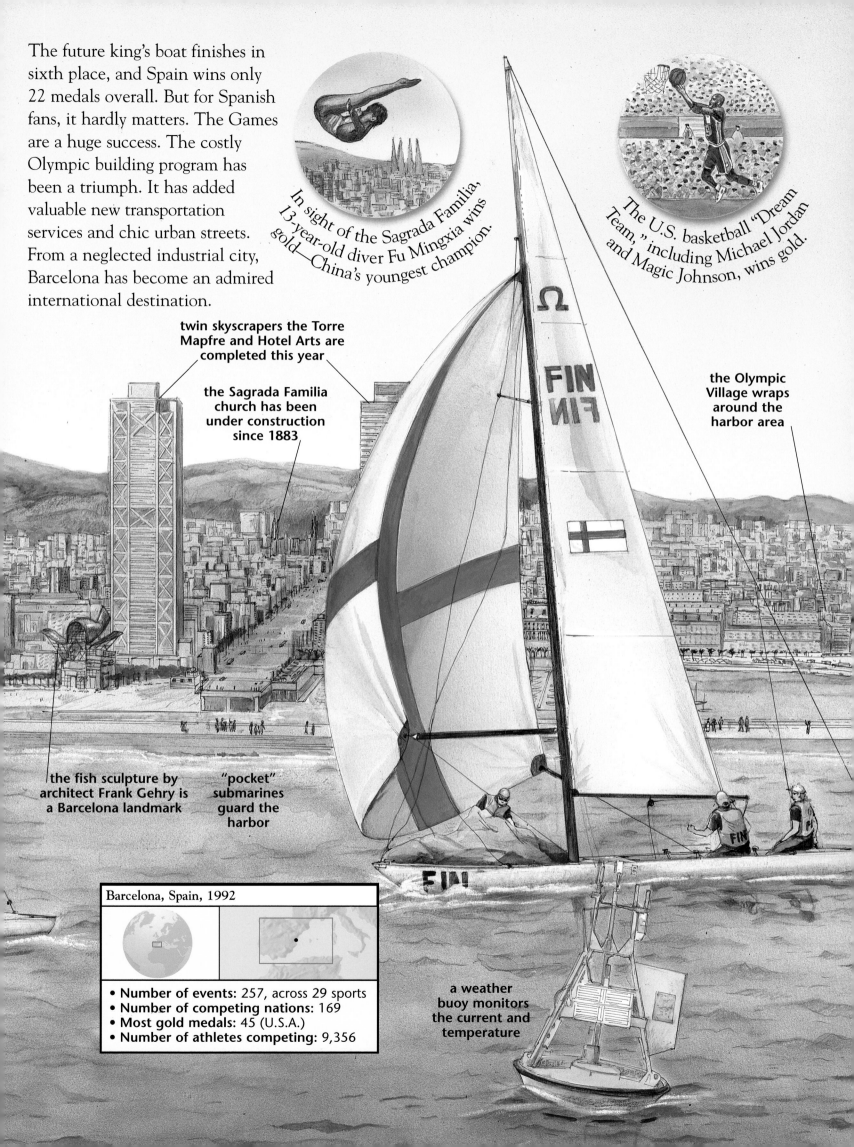

The future king's boat finishes in sixth place, and Spain wins only 22 medals overall. But for Spanish fans, it hardly matters. The Games are a huge success. The costly Olympic building program has been a triumph. It has added valuable new transportation services and chic urban streets. From a neglected industrial city, Barcelona has become an admired international destination.

In sight of the Sagrada Familia, 13-year-old diver Fu Mingxia wins gold—China's youngest champion.

The U.S. basketball "Dream Team," including Michael Jordan and Magic Johnson, wins gold.

twin skyscrapers the Torre Mapfre and Hotel Arts are completed this year

the Sagrada Familia church has been under construction since 1883

the Olympic Village wraps around the harbor area

the fish sculpture by architect Frank Gehry is a Barcelona landmark

"pocket" submarines guard the harbor

a weather buoy monitors the current and temperature

Barcelona, Spain, 1992

- **Number of events:** 257, across 29 sports
- **Number of competing nations:** 169
- **Most gold medals:** 45 (U.S.A.)
- **Number of athletes competing:** 9,356

Lillehammer 1994

In Europe's icy north, the season for sports has always been the winter. So almost as soon as the Olympics began, Scandinavian people demanded that the Games include their favorite contests on ice and snow. Some early Games featured ice skating, but a full Winter Olympics started only in 1924, in Chamonix, France. The results were no surprise: Finland, Norway, Austria, and Switzerland won almost every event!

Seventy years later, the Norwegian town of Lillehammer is the host for the 17th Winter Olympics. Snowbound for five months of the year—and only 370 mi. (600km) from the Arctic Circle—it is the ideal setting. The nail-biting highlight of the Games comes on the last day, with the men's slalom. The contestants ski the slalom course twice, and their times are added together to choose the winner.

Lillehammer, Norway, 1994

- Number of events: 61, across 12 sports
- Number of competing nations: 67
- Most gold medals: 11 (Russia)
- Number of athletes competing: 1,737

competitors must ski between paired flags called gates

the course includes both wide and narrow gates

skiers must cross the slope as well as going straight down

alternate gate pairs are colored blue and red

at least one-fourth of the course is on steep, 30-degree (1-in-3) slopes

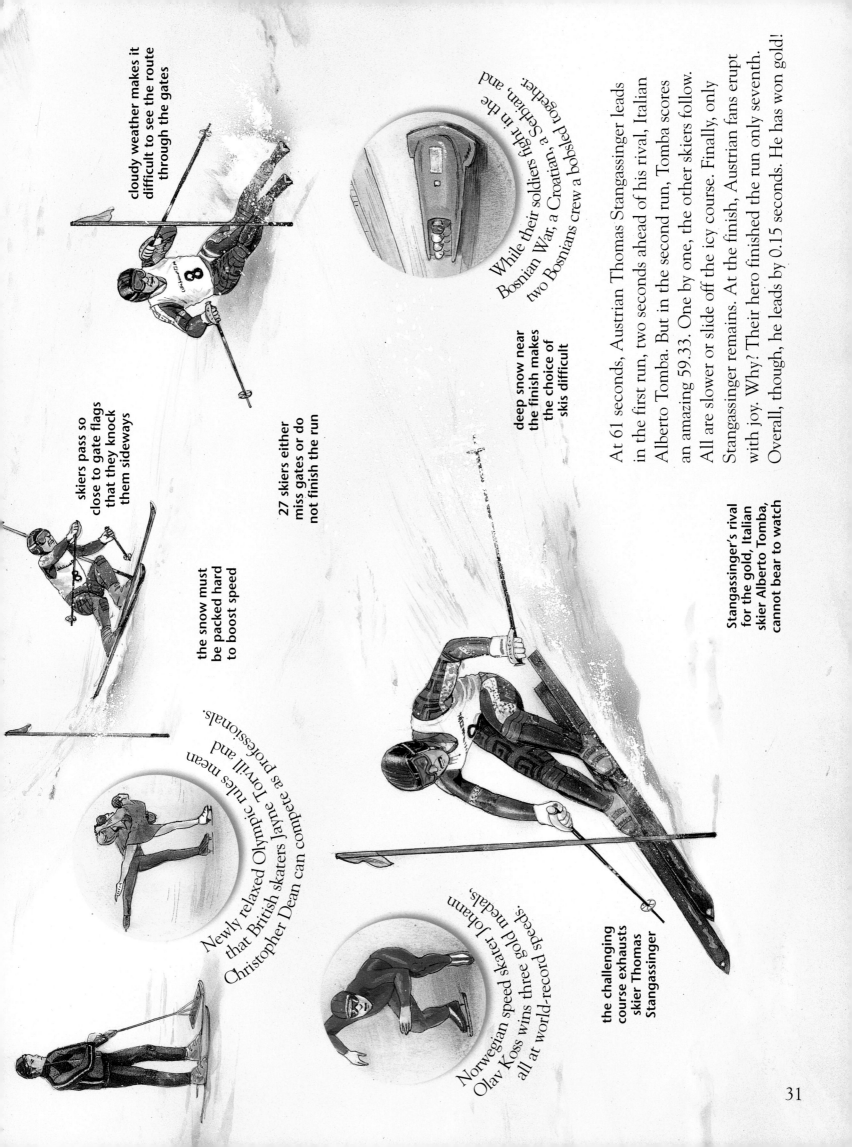

cloudy weather makes it difficult to see the route through the gates

skiers pass so close to gate flags that they knock them sideways

27 skiers either miss gates or do not finish the run

the snow must be packed hard to boost speed

While their soldiers fight in the Bosnian War, a Croatian, a Serbian, and two Bosnians crew a bobsled together.

deep snow near the finish makes the choice of skis difficult

Stangassinger's rival for the gold, Italian skier Alberto Tomba, cannot bear to watch

the challenging course exhausts skier Thomas Stangassinger

Newly relaxed Olympic rules mean that British skaters Jayne Torvill and Christopher Dean can compete as professionals.

Norwegian speed skater Johann Olav Koss wins three gold medals, all at world-record speeds.

At 61 seconds, Austrian Thomas Stangassinger leads in the first run, two seconds ahead of his rival, Italian Alberto Tomba. But in the second run, Tomba scores an amazing 59.33. One by one, the other skiers follow. All are slower or slide off the icy course. Finally, only Stangassinger remains. At the finish, Austrian fans erupt with joy. Why? Their hero finished the run only seventh. Overall, though, he leads by 0.15 seconds. He has won gold!

Atlanta 1996

After only 12 years, the Games return to the U.S. Americans are delighted that Atlanta is hosting the Olympics, but they are cautious of the cost. They need not worry: sponsors and TV companies quickly pledge enough to pay for the Games. Other nations are not so pleased. Competition to host the Olympics is as hot as the rivalry on the track.

American Michael Johnson's double Olympic gold in the 200m and the 400m is a feat no athlete has yet equaled.

Atlanta, Georgia, U.S., 1996

- **Number of events:** 271, across 31 sports
- **Number of competing nations:** 197
- **Most gold medals:** 44 (U.S.A.)
- **Number of athletes competing:** 10,318

Lewis takes victory on his third jump and declines to jump again

the jump is short of Lewis's best but is still enough to win

Lewis's main rivals, Mike Powell (U.S.A.) and Ivan Pedroso (Cuba), are handicapped by injuries

Discontent gets worse when the Games open. Transportation is crowded, vital computers break down, volunteers struggle to help visitors, and messages from sponsors are loud and intrusive. But as the races begin and records start to fall, all of this is forgotten. On July 29, when Carl Lewis lines up for the long jump, it seems like everyone in the stadium is holding their breath.

Lewis is 35 years old, and this will be his last Olympics. But he looks confident and happy as he starts his third jump. He takes 21 long, loping strides and arcs through the air. He falls forward in the sand. The scoreboard flashes 8.50 meters (27 ft. 10 3/4 in.)! It is not his best, but it is enough to win. Lewis throws up his arms. This is his ninth gold medal: a triumphant end to an amazing career.

French sprinter Marie-José Pérec wins the women's 200m and then takes the 400-m gold in world-record time.

the stadium will be converted to a baseball park after the Olympics

judges check for foul jumps and measure length

the stadium is almost full to capacity for the final

in the earlier trials, Lewis was within a few centimeters (about an inch) of not qualifying for the final

after the jumps, Lewis jogs a victory lap carrying two American flags— and takes away a bag of sand from the pit as a souvenir

athletes whose feet illegally cross the takeoff line leave footprints on the clay strip

the sand is raked flat after each jump

Spanish cyclist Miguel Indurain wins the 52-km individual time trial by a margin of only 12 seconds.

In the 100m, Canadian Donovan Bailey sets a new world record, at 9.84 seconds.

33

Sydney 2000

As the 20th century ends, the Olympic movement is in trouble. News reports focus on everything that goes wrong. Athletes take drugs. Officials accept bribes. Sponsors make big profits. But then Sydney's success silences the critics. Australia's biggest, brightest city puts on a Games that everyone agrees are well organized, joyful, honest, and fair.

The women's marathon sums up the Sydney spirit. Its route aims to give as many people as possible a "free ticket" to the Olympics. Families on the course paint their houses and hold marathon barbecues. For the 53 competitors, though, the race is deadly serious. It is a showcase for the strength and determination of female athletes. Naoko Takahashi of Japan, who takes the gold medal, beats the winning time of 13 previous men's marathons.

the famous Sydney Opera House is the starting point for the triathlon

Sydney's vast natural harbor is the perfect setting for sailing races

the marathon commemorates 100 years of women's Olympic participation

Australian Ian Thorpe — "the Thorpedo"—takes two gold medals and sets a world record, all in one hour.

the winner is Naoko Takahashi of Japan

British rower Steve Redgrave's win makes him one of only four people to win gold in five straight Olympics.

around 47,000 volunteers make sure everything runs smoothly

a test event in April tried out the course

spectators offer to buy volunteers' uniforms as souvenirs

Sydney, Australia, 2000

- **Number of events:** 300, across 28 sports
- **Number of competing nations:** 199
- **Most gold medals:** 37 (U.S.A.)
- **Number of athletes competing:** 10,651

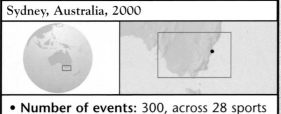

press photographers ride in special trucks

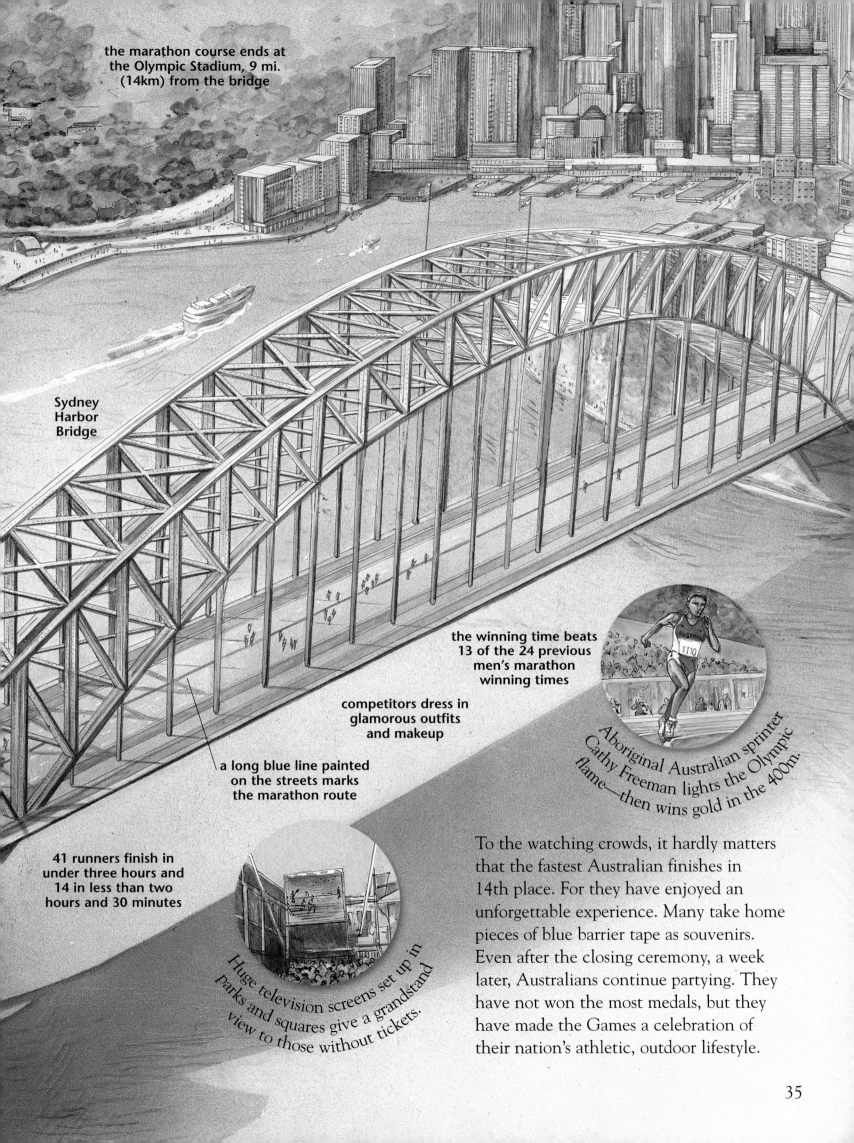

the marathon course ends at the Olympic Stadium, 9 mi. (14km) from the bridge

Sydney Harbor Bridge

the winning time beats 13 of the 24 previous men's marathon winning times

competitors dress in glamorous outfits and makeup

a long blue line painted on the streets marks the marathon route

Aboriginal Australian sprinter Cathy Freeman lights the Olympic flame—then wins gold in the 400m.

41 runners finish in under three hours and 14 in less than two hours and 30 minutes

Huge television screens set up in parks and squares give a grandstand view to those without tickets.

To the watching crowds, it hardly matters that the fastest Australian finishes in 14th place. For they have enjoyed an unforgettable experience. Many take home pieces of blue barrier tape as souvenirs. Even after the closing ceremony, a week later, Australians continue partying. They have not won the most medals, but they have made the Games a celebration of their nation's athletic, outdoor lifestyle.

35

Athens 2004

The ancient home of the Olympics is host to the Games once more—more than 1,600 years after sports ended here in Olympia. Greece's rulers banned the Games as pagan (un-Christian) in the A.D. 300s and destroyed the shrines where runners saluted the ancient gods. However, the long, flat track survived. Putting the Olympics back in Olympia has involved some changes: today, women take part and athletes no longer compete naked!

Kelly Holmes becomes the first British woman since 1912 to take two gold medals at the same Games.

athletes compete exactly where the Olympics began, 2,800 years ago

the stadium is almost unchanged since ancient times

shot is a simple metal ball the size of a small melon

the simple staging aims to preserve the atmosphere of the ancient venue

simple cards show the scores

athletes must not step outside the circle

Yuriy Bilonog (Ukraine) takes gold with a 21.16-m throw

After winning both the 1,500-m and 5,000-m races, Moroccan runner Hicham El Guerrouj dances with joy.

In many other ways, though, little is different. Spectators again watch from grassy banks, for Greece's archaeologists protect Olympia fiercely. They have outlawed buildings, seats, lights, and electronic scoreboards. The only event permitted here is the one judged least likely to damage this historic monument: the shot put.

most people do not have actual seats and sit on grassy slopes

a sloping ridge gives spectators a better view

Athens, Greece, 2004

- **Number of events:** 301, across 34 sports
- **Number of competing nations:** 201
- **Most gold medals:** 36 (U.S.A.)
- **Number of athletes competing:** 10,625

U.S.A. swimmer Michael Phelps wins six gold and two bronze medals, topping the table in Athens.

Argentina's soccer players defeat Paraguay, winning their first gold in 52 years—watched by 44,000 people.

judges wave a white flag for a fair throw

a red flag signals a foul throw

It is not normally a popular event, but today, 18,000 spectators have traveled four hours from Athens, which is hosting the other events. The capital sparkles for the Games, with slick transportation systems and grand new stadiums. But here, in the heat and dust, centuries slip away. As the shot-putters jostle for gold, the ghosts of ancient Olympians look on.

Beijing 2008

In China's ancient capital, the most lavish Olympics ever are reaching a peak of excitement. China's rulers have organized these Games with military precision. They want nothing to spoil the picture of fairness and athletic skill in the stadium, so 100,000 volunteers mingle with the spectators to ensure that only sports makes the news.

The Olympic Stadium is called the "bird's nest" because of its oval shape and twiglike structure.

Bolt's shoes have golden spikes on the soles

Beijing, China, 2008

- **Number of events:** 302, across 34 sports
- **Number of competing nations:** 204
- **Most gold medals:** 51 (China)
- **Number of athletes competing:** 10,942

paramedics stand by in case of injury to the athletes

civilian security personnel mingle with the crowd

the Jamaican flag covers Bolt's shoulders for the victory lap

Olympic judges watch the start to ensure fairness

Chinese soldiers help keep order

a technician checks the anemometer, which measures wind speed

track crews prepare the running surface and equipment

the track is rubber coated, with a high-grip surface for speed and safety

Today, August 16, every camera lens is pointing at Usain Bolt. The 21-year-old Jamaican has already broken world sprinting records. Now, he is the favorite to win the 100m. He does not let the crowd down. After a shaky start, he surges into the lead. Sixty-five feet (20m) from the finish, he is so sure of winning that he slows down and beats his chest in triumph!

Trackside cameras show Bolt crossing the finishing line an amazing 6.5 ft. (2m) ahead of his rivals.

Chris Hoy leads the British team to scoop seven of the 11 gold medals in track cycling events.

Two billion people worldwide watch the televised opening ceremony, featuring 15,000 performers.

press photographers jostle to capture Bolt's celebration pose

a video cameraman balances on a two-wheeled Segway cart

a timekeeping expert monitors the photo-finish camera

at 6 ft. 5 in. (195cm), Bolt is the tallest man ever to win the 100m

if Bolt's shoelaces had not become untied, he would have run even faster!

It is an extraordinary win, even by Olympic standards: wind gauges show zero, so Bolt won without any help from a breeze, and his left shoelace came untied during the race. Bolt completes a victory lap and then poses for pictures near the scoreboard that shows his record time of 9.69 seconds. In four days he will win again, in the 200m. No wonder his nickname is "Lightning" Bolt.

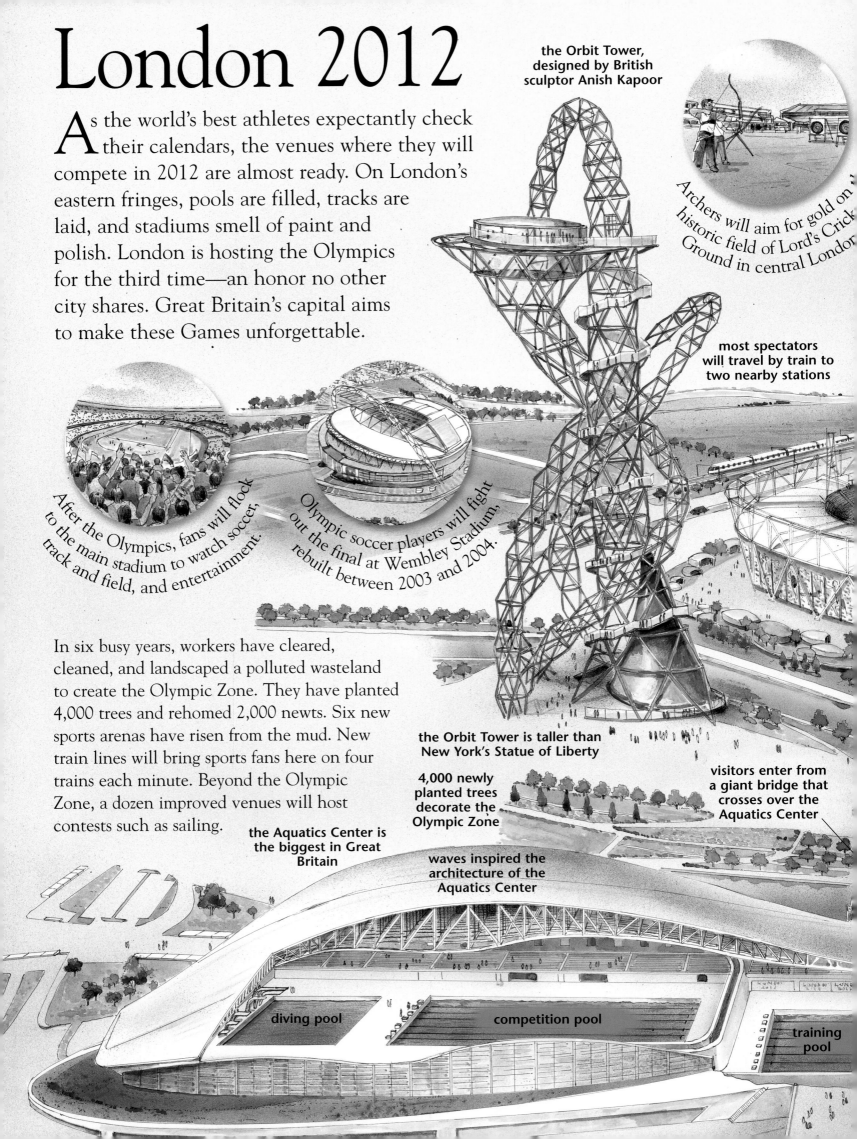

London 2012

As the world's best athletes expectantly check their calendars, the venues where they will compete in 2012 are almost ready. On London's eastern fringes, pools are filled, tracks are laid, and stadiums smell of paint and polish. London is hosting the Olympics for the third time—an honor no other city shares. Great Britain's capital aims to make these Games unforgettable.

In six busy years, workers have cleared, cleaned, and landscaped a polluted wasteland to create the Olympic Zone. They have planted 4,000 trees and rehomed 2,000 newts. Six new sports arenas have risen from the mud. New train lines will bring sports fans here on four trains each minute. Beyond the Olympic Zone, a dozen improved venues will host contests such as sailing.

the Orbit Tower, designed by British sculptor Anish Kapoor

Archers will aim for gold on the historic field of Lord's Cricket Ground in central London

most spectators will travel by train to two nearby stations

After the Olympics, fans will flock to the main stadium to watch soccer, track and field, and entertainment.

Olympic soccer players will fight out the final at Wembley Stadium, rebuilt between 2003 and 2004.

the Orbit Tower is taller than New York's Statue of Liberty

4,000 newly planted trees decorate the Olympic Zone

visitors enter from a giant bridge that crosses over the Aquatics Center

the Aquatics Center is the biggest in Great Britain

waves inspired the architecture of the Aquatics Center

diving pool

competition pool

training pool

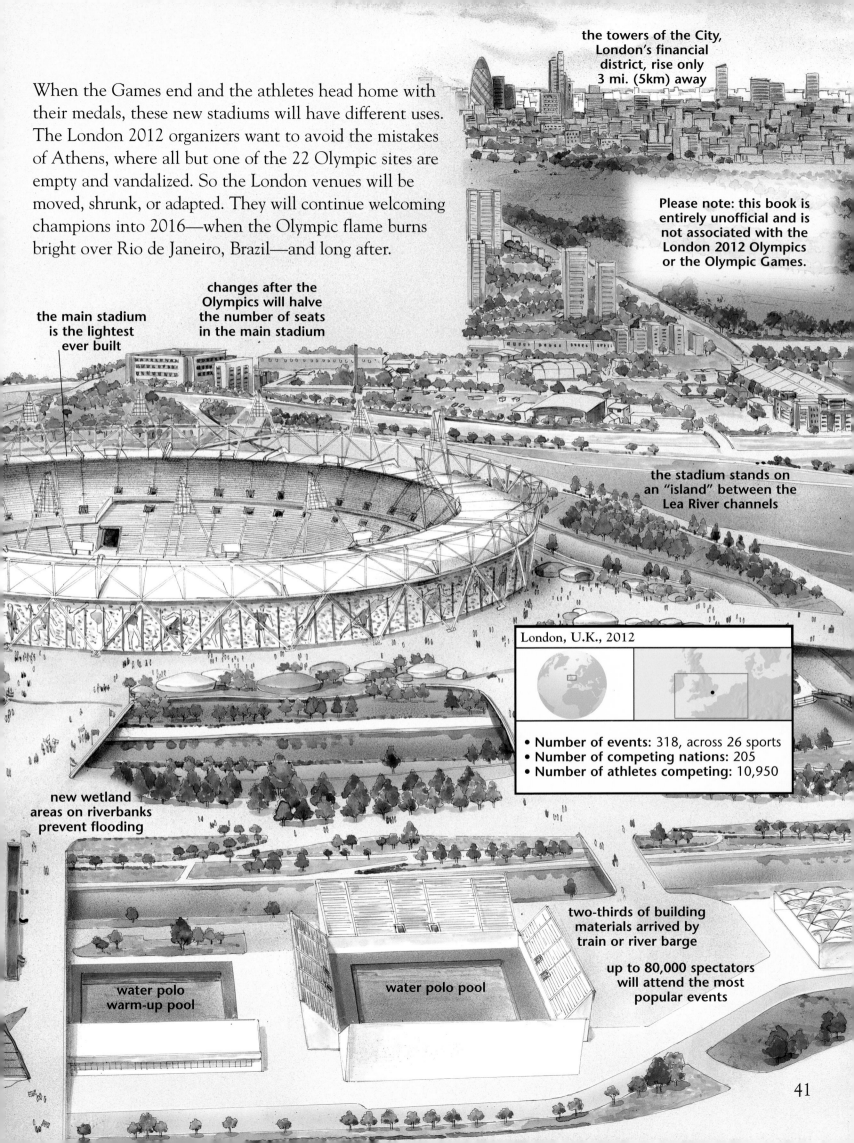

When the Games end and the athletes head home with their medals, these new stadiums will have different uses. The London 2012 organizers want to avoid the mistakes of Athens, where all but one of the 22 Olympic sites are empty and vandalized. So the London venues will be moved, shrunk, or adapted. They will continue welcoming champions into 2016—when the Olympic flame burns bright over Rio de Janeiro, Brazil—and long after.

the towers of the City, London's financial district, rise only 3 mi. (5km) away

Please note: this book is entirely unofficial and is not associated with the London 2012 Olympics or the Olympic Games.

changes after the Olympics will halve the number of seats in the main stadium

the main stadium is the lightest ever built

the stadium stands on an "island" between the Lea River channels

London, U.K., 2012

- Number of events: 318, across 26 sports
- Number of competing nations: 205
- Number of athletes competing: 10,950

new wetland areas on riverbanks prevent flooding

water polo warm-up pool

water polo pool

two-thirds of building materials arrived by train or river barge

up to 80,000 spectators will attend the most popular events

Facts and records

1896 Athens, Greece *see page 7*
In this first modern Games, Greek runner Spyridon Louis takes the marathon title, watched by 100,000 people. Winners in all events receive a silver medal and an olive branch.

1900 Paris, France *see page 8*
Constantin de Zubiera becomes the first black medalist when France wins the tug of war. Alvin Kraenzlein (U.S.A.) wins the 60-m, 110-m, and 200-m hurdles and the long jump.

1904 St. Louis, Missouri, U.S.
Transportation problems mean that only 12 nations take part. Americans win 239 of the 280 medals, which for the first time are gold, silver, and bronze. Ray Ewry (U.S.A.) wins the high, long, and triple jumps.

1908 London, U.K.
Great Britain wins 56 gold medals, a feat the country has not achieved since. Italian marathon winner Dorando Pietri is disqualified after officials help him finish the race.

1912 Stockholm, Sweden
Competitors from all inhabited continents take part for the first time. Finnish runner Hannes Kolehmainen takes gold in the 5-km, 10-km, and 12-km crosscountry.

Steve Ovett and Sebastian Coe competing in Moscow in 1980

1920 Antwerp, Belgium
Doves are released for the first time at the opening ceremony. Swede Oscar Swahn, 72, wins silver in the shooting event known as the 100-m "running deer," to become the oldest Olympic medalist. Italian Nedo Nadi takes five fencing golds.

1924 Paris, France
Finnish distance runner Paavo Nurmi takes five golds, three in individual events and two in one hour. Twenty-three gymnasts score a perfect 10 in rope climbing.

1928 Amsterdam, Netherlands
The Olympic flame is lit for the first time. American swimmer Johnny Weissmuller, who later becomes a movie star, wins two golds. New rules mean women can compete in gymnastics and track-and-field events, doubling athlete numbers.

American swimmer Mark Spitz left the 1972 Olympics with seven gold medals.

1932 Los Angeles, California, U.S.
Athletes stay in the first Olympic Village. American Mildred "Babe" Didrikson wins medals in the high jump, hurdles, and javelin. During the Olympic trials, she had also won at the long jump, shot put, and baseball throw!

1936 Berlin, Germany *see page 10*
African-American athlete Jesse Owens takes four gold medals, to the dismay of the watching Nazi leaders. Nevertheless, Germany leads the medals table, with 89 in total.

1948 London, U.K. *see page 12*
Rivals dismiss Fanny Blankers-Koen as "too old," yet the 30-year-old Dutch runner wins four golds. At 17, Bob Mathias (U.S.A.) is the youngest gold medalist ever on the track.

1952 Helsinki, Finland
Emil Zátopek, nicknamed "the Czech locomotive," takes gold and Olympic records at the 5,000m and 10,000m. At the last minute, he enters the marathon —which he has never run before—and wins it.

1956 Melbourne, Australia
In the first Olympics in the Southern Hemisphere, the host nation wins all of the freestyle swimming events. A defeated American accuses them of professionalism (Olympic rules ban paid athletes).

1960 Rome, Italy *see page 14*
Aged only 18, boxer Cassius Clay (who later

renamed himself Muhammad Ali) wins the light heavyweight final. Victory earns him one of the 34 gold medals taken home by the U.S.A. team.

1964 Tokyo, Japan *see page 16*
By adding six more medals to the 12 she already holds, Soviet gymnast Larissa Latynina scoops the record for the most Olympic medals of any athlete.

1968 Mexico City, Mexico *see page 18*
In the highest Games so far (7,380 ft., or 2,250m, above sea level), the thin air helps athletes sprint and leap to victory. World records fall at the 100m, 200m, and 400m; the 100-m and 400-m relay; and long and triple jumps.

1972 Munich, West Germany *see page 20*
With five medals and three world records, 15-year-old swimmer Shane Gould is an Australian hero—but he is overshadowed by American Mark Spitz, who wins seven golds.

Host nation Japan swept the judo medals table in 1964.

1976 Montreal, Canada
Billion-dollar debts and no gold medals make the Games a disaster for Canada. But for Romanian gymnast Nadia Comaneci, Montreal is a triumph. She scores a perfect 10—seven times over.

1980 Moscow, Soviet Union *see page 22*
Though a boycott removes some of the world's best athletes, those who do come to Moscow perform well. Together, they break 34 world records and 62 Olympic records.

1984 Los Angeles, California, U.S. *see page 24*
American Carl Lewis takes the gold medal in the 100-m and 200-m sprints, the long jump, and the 100-m relay—repeating Jesse Owens's legendary performance in Berlin in 1936.

1988 Seoul, South Korea *see page 26*
While the world watches a drugs scandal unfold, Kenyan runners quietly scoop up the long-distance medals on the track, winning gold in the 800m, 1,500m, and 5,000m and in the 3-km steeplechase.

1992 Barcelona, Spain *see page 28*
When Chris Boardman (Great Britain) pedals to victory in the 400-m pursuit, rivals credit his high-tech, carbon-fiber bicycle. But he later proves it was the rider who won gold by breaking records on regular bikes.

1996 Atlanta, Georgia, U.S. *see page 32*
Michelle Smith becomes Ireland's most successful Olympic athlete by winning three gold medals and one bronze in the swimming pool. Of the 197 nations competing in Atlanta, 79 win medals—an Olympic record.

2000 Sydney, Australia *see page 34*
By winning two gold medals, Australian swimmer Ian Thorpe becomes an instant hero. The following day, his portrait appears on a postage stamp.

2004 Athens, Greece *see page 36*
The marathon leader, Brazilian Vanderlei de Lima, is dragged from the track by an Irish priest 6 mi. (10km) from the end. He finishes only third—but gets a special sportsmanship prize.

2008 Beijing, China *see page 38*
An extraordinary effort by China's athletes enables the host nation to top the gold-medal table, with 51 firsts. Their greatest successes are in gymnastics events, in which they win 18 medals.

Nazi leader Adolf Hitler watched as Jesse Owens took gold in the men's 100m in Berlin in 1936.

Glossary

Words in *italics* refer to other glossary entries.

Arctic Circle
An imaginary circle around the northern tip of Earth, within which the sun never sets on at least one summer day each year.

atomic bomb
A very powerful bomb that causes sickness and death even long after it explodes.

Aztecs
Native Central-American people who ruled Mexico between the A.D. 1300s and 1500s.

barracks
Living accommodation for soldiers.

basilica
A building, usually found next to a *forum* in ancient Roman cities.

bathhouse
An ancient Roman building where the public could wash, take baths, and exercise.

Bosnian War
A three-year war in the 1990s in which Serb and Croat people fought for control of the eastern European state of Bosnia and Herzegovina.

bout
An organized boxing or wrestling match that forms part of a bigger competition.

boycott
A way of protesting by not buying or using a product or service.

bribe
An illegal payment made to obtain a favor from someone with power or authority.

The first modern Games, in 1896, were held in sight of the ancient Parthenon in Athens, Greece.

civil rights movement
A campaign between 1950 and 1980 to obtain equal treatment for all citizens, no matter what their race or religion might be.

Ancient Olympian athletes were awarded laurel crowns rather than medals.

Cold War
The period between 1947 and 1991 when the Soviet Union and the United States feared and mistrusted each other but did not openly fight.

emperor
A ruler who controls a large region and who has complete power over its people.

Exposition Universelle
One of a series of grand fairs held in Paris, France, celebrating achievements in art and science.

forum
The marketplace and central open space of an ancient Roman town.

freestyle
A race in which contestants choose how to compete, rather than being restricted to a single style, such as breaststroke in a swimming race.

gladiator
A slave trained to fight in combats staged in an ancient Roman amphitheater.

Greco-Roman wrestling
A wrestling competition based on the style that may have been popular in ancient Greece and Rome.

guerrilla
A volunteer soldier who fights outside of a regular army, often for a cause in which he or she strongly believes.

hostage
A prisoner whose captors demand money or promises in exchange for his or her release.

lynch
To execute illegally, without trial, often in public.

marathon
A long running race of just over 26 mi. (42km).

Nazi
The political party that ruled Germany (1933–1945) under the complete control of its leader, Adolf Hitler.

OPHR
The Olympic Project for Human Rights, a part of the U.S. *civil rights movement* that aimed to end racism in sports and the Olympics.

pagan
A name given by Christians to those who do not share their religion.

Paralympics*
A sporting competition for disabled athletes, held after each Olympic Games.

*Note: the term *Paralympics* is a protected mark of the Olympic Games.*

Parthenon
A famous temple in the Acropolis, the ancient hilltop city at the heart of Athens, Greece.

peddler
A merchant who travels around selling goods to homes or at fairs and markets.

podium
A raised platform: in the Olympics, a stepped platform on which medalists stand.

propane
A gas fuel that is sometimes used to create the Olympic flame.

racism
The mistaken belief that people of one race or skin color are better than another.

ration
A small amount of food, just enough to feed someone for one day.

refugee camp
A temporary home for people driven from their land or homes by war, famine, or disaster.

the marathon in Paris in 1900

relay
A team race in which each member completes only one stage of the overall course.

satellite
A natural or artificial object, such as a machine, that constantly circles Earth.

scaffolding
A temporary framework on which workers can stand while constructing a building.

slalom
A winding, zigzag course marked by poles.

sniper
A stealthy killer who shoots from a hiding place.

Soling
A type of small yacht, with a crew of three, in which Olympic sailors competed from 1972 to 2000.

Soviet Union (U.S.S.R.)
The alliance of Russia and surrounding states that together formed one of the world's greatest nations between 1922 and 1991.

sponsor
A person or company that provides support in the form of promises, help, or money.

terrorist
Someone who seeks power by frightening others with acts or threats of violence and crime.

A Spanish prince took part in the Olympic Soling race in 1992.

Index

The men's 100-m sprint final at the Seoul Games in 1988.

KINGFISHER
LONDON & NEW YORK

Distributed in the U.S. and Canada by Macmillan,
175 Fifth Ave., New York, NY 10010

With thanks to:
Sue Verhoef at the Atlanta History Center, Atlanta, Georgia
Caroline Lam—British Olympic Committee archivist
Omega Timing

With special thanks to Anish Kapoor for the reproduction of his Orbit Tower design (page 40):
Orbit, 2010
Anish Kapoor
In collaboration with Cecil Balmond, ARUP

Additional illustration work by Monica Favilli and Cecilia Scutti

Created for Kingfisher by White-Thomson Publishing Ltd.
www.wtpub.co.uk

Library of Congress Cataloging-in-Publication data has been applied for.

ISBN 978-0-7534-6710-7 (HC)
ISBN 978-0-7534-6868-5 (PB)

Kingfisher books are available for special promotions and premiums.
For details contact: Special Markets Department, Macmillan,
175 Fifth Avenue, New York, NY 10010.

For more information, please visit www.kingfisherbooks.com

Printed in China
1 3 5 7 9 8 6 4 2

1TR/1111/WKT/UNTD/140MA

Mary Lou Retton scored a perfect 10 in gymnastics at the 1984 Olympics in Los Angeles, California.